STORIES FROM CHINA

Home of Giant Pandas and Crested Ibises

Cui Lili

Foreign Languages Press

First Edition 2007

ISBN 978-7-119-05158-1
Foreign Languages Press, Beijing, China, 2007
Published by Foreign Languages Press
24 Baiwanzhuang Road, Beijing 100037, China
Website: http: //www.flp.com.cn
Email Addresses: Info@flp.com.cn
Sales@flp.com.cn
Distributed by China International Book Trading Corporation
35 Chegongzhuang Xilu, Beijing 100044, China
P. O. Box 399, Beijing, China

Printed in the People's Republic of China

Contents

Home of Giant Pandas and Crested Ibises

Foreword

"In the Qinling Mountains all things on earth come back to life in the month of March.

"In the dense forests of Shaanxi's Foping State Nature Reserve, located at 1,700 meters above sea level, oak trees with bare trunks reach toward the skies, desiring to drink in the growth energy radi-

▼ A bird's-eye view of Qinling Mountains

ating from the sun… Meanwhile news of the arrival of spring is spreading in whispers among the buds of the rose family. An alert squirrel, with a mushroom clutched to its bosom, shoots up a tree. Its actions alarm a nuthatch hopping up and down the branches looking for food. The bird suddenly vanishes.

"All is quiet in the valley except for our own footfalls and the gurgling of the stream. From time to time we hear the sweet twittering of sure-footed bush warblers from the opposite mountain slope… It sounds as if from somewhere nearby, further setting off the tranquility of the high mountains. Through the underbrush in the forest, several impatient golden pheasants are whooshing up and down, the males chasing after the females. They display their gorgeous wings and ruffle their vivid feathers showing off the best of their skill. The spectacle resembles bounding balls of flame. Consequently a mood of restlessness inspired by the dancing birds begins to spread through the forest.

"In sharp contrast to the bare-trunk, sharp-edged oaks, lower in the deep forest can be found a grove of Bashan bamboo growing luxuriantly. In early spring this plant form makes for the most beautiful scene in the forest area of the Qinling Mountains.

"A Chinese fir tree stretches out sturdy branches from a steep slope. In the distance we suddenly catch sight of a giant panda lying lazily in the tree. We try to contain our wild joy, and carefully pussyfoot closer, in hopes of finding a suitable angle for getting a good shot... For all our caution, the creature sniffed something out and nimbly drops to the ground. Then it fades away unhurriedly into the bamboo grove, leaving no chance for us to take any photos....

"Not knowing how much time had elapsed, we all of a sudden hear noises made by the fighting of giant pandas from the other side of the slope. It sounds like the howling of wolfhounds, but much louder and clearer, reverberating all over the valley. With all our energy we push down the slope, trying to make our way through overlapping layers of bamboo. At the bottom of the valley we advance swiftly towards our target along the path already treaded out by the giant mammals. Sure enough, we can hear rustlings from the bamboo grove below the trees. Guided by the sounds, we scan ahead and catch sight of one, two, three, and then four pandas. Then we realize there's another one lying very close to us. This is how we found at least five male pandas under a tree in which one female was crouching above us...."

Guan Ke, director of the Information and Pro-
motion Center under the Forestry Department of
Shaanxi Province, told us the above story that he
had personally experienced in a Qinling forest three
years ago. Then he continued: "Even with my years
of experience in field photography, I'd never before found myself face to face with more than two
giant pandas at one time. Moreover, it's a rare sight
to see a group fighting over a female panda in spring
heat."

Growing up at the foot of the Qinling Mountains, Guan Ke, face burnished by a life outdoors,
has a pithy style of conversation. Nourished by the
striking scenery around him, of elegiac mountains
and streams, he possesses a natural literary talent.
He pours out deep emotions from the Qinling
Mountains and expresses it in his writings, so that
every reader can share his joy and amazement. He
seems blessed each time he goes into the depths of
the mountain forests with his camera, as if the
mountain range, understanding his intentions, displays before him innumerous kinds of animals and
plants, such as giant pandas, crested ibis, golden
monkeys, takin, tufted deer, and more. This is the
same mountain range that has quietly protected all
of these life forms for thousands of years.

1

Qinling Mountains: Habitats
of Rare Animals

Located in the middle of China's territory, Qinling is the highest and longest mountain range running from west to east. It is seen by geographers as the demarcation line between northern and southern China; while zoologists take it as the dividing line between Gubei and Dongyang, where the two completely different regions of biodiversity converge; and meteorologists regard Qinling as the transition area between the northern subtropical zone and the warm temperate zone... However, for all the diversity of natural life that have made it their home, the Qinling Mountains is the habitat best suited for their survival. There they live and procreate generation after generation. In return, to the mountains' unique environment they bestow their wild colors, extremely sweet birdsong, creating a scene of vital beauty.

A Miraculous Mountain Range

The orogenic shifting of the Himalayas, 80 million years ago or even later, formed the Qinling mountain range. According to plate tectonics theory, the Qinling orogenic zone was produced by the meeting of the southern continental edge of the North China plate and the northern continental edge of the Yangtze plate. The collision of the two huge plates caused the two edges to rise and formed the magnificent Qinling mountain landforms of today.

Like a dragon lying across the center of China, the mountain range has become the most important north-south demarcation line in the country's physical geography as well as cultural and human geography. Composed of several parallel mountain chains with valleys and basins in between, it has an altitude from 1,500 to over 3,000 meters on average. To its north is the Weihe River, the largest tributary of the Yellow River, and to its south flows the Hanjiang River, the largest tributary of the Yangtze. Thus, it also forms the watershed between the Yellow River and the Yangtze — the two largest rivers in China.

Due to the differences in power between the inner sides and outer sides during its orogeny, the features of the landforms on each side of the range are quite distinct. Gentle on the southern slopes, the mountain range meanders with ridges and peaks rising one after another. Distributed in their midst are terraces and basins. The northern slopes are

▼ Quaternary Glaciation in Qinling

▲ Flowers blooming over the Qinling Mountains

precipitous, hundreds of peaks rising steeply with cliffs, each vying with the other for charm. Mount Taibai, the highest peak of the Qinling, along with the famed Mount Zhongnan, Mount Huashan and others, are all located on the northern slopes.

In meteorology, the east-west run of the Qinling mountains constitutes a natural protective screen. In winter, it blocks the northwesterly winds from blowing down to the south, allowing fewer cold currents to hit the area on its southern side. In summer, it shelters the Central Shaanxi Plains and the region to its north, from rain clouds brought by air currents from the southeast. As a result the climates of the northern side and the southern side of the range are widely dissimilar. The northern side is a warm temperate zone with a semi-moist climate, quite distinct from the northern subtropical moist climate of the southern side. In the third lunar month in spring, the southern region displays scenes of golden canola fields. Bees busily shuttle among pink and white broad-bean flowers and pea flowers of red alternating with white. Green seedlings grow healthily in paddy fields. All the mountains and plains are adorned with views of luxuriance, embellished with crimson peach and snow-white apricot blossoms. In contrast, the Central Shaanxi Plains, located to the north of the range, provide a picture of dry-land cultivation. Wheat grows in spring, while maize is the summer crop. Poplar and willow trees line both sides of the roads, and apple trees can be seen everywhere in gardens.

Not a few people believe that Qinling is a miraculous mountain range. According to records, the Qinling Mountains and the Central Shaanxi Plains on the northern side of the range occupy an important position in the development of Chinese history. This place is the cradle of the Chinese nation. At least 13 historical dynasties built their capitals there. Zhou, Qin, Han and Tang—the four major unified dynasties in the early half of Chinese history—advanced Chinese culture to levels of great prosperity in the same region. However, at the same time, the local ecological environment was also brought to ruin by unending wars, frequent changes of dynasties, and extortionate demands on Nature after the growth of the population. For this we have paid dearly.

In modern times, especially in the last few decades, the productive standard of humankind has developed at astonishing speeds. In terms of Nature, the repercussions of production have often gone beyond the human imagination. In the wake of agricultural civilization, waves of industrial civilization have swept across the world. The global ecosystem has changed beyond recognition. "However, Qinling is an exception," said Guan Ke. As an officer of the Forestry Department he expressed his views with apparent emotion. "This mountain range has the closest relationship with the most flourishing ancient culture of human society. Again and again it suffered serious destruction and damage. It still maintains its primitive natural ecology, presenting the image of a wild emerald. It has placed all creatures under its protection, and is still listed as one of the world's 11 essential areas of biodiversity. It is a living miracle."

Paradise of Fauna and Flora

Today, in the high mountains and dense forests of the Qinling Mountains, co-existing with China's national treasure, the giant panda, are also found innumerable mammals including serow, wild boars, black bears, musk deer, hedgehogs, bamboo rats, etc. In addition to what have been identified as clouded leopard, jackal, yellow-throated marten, leopard cat and other species of carnivorous animals, Chinese zoologists have never given up hope in looking for the South China tiger. And flying side by side in the skies with the rare bird, the crested ibis, known as a "gem of the East," are the black storks, a state first-class protected bird, and pheasants, part of the most bounteous bird community in the world. Viewed from afar, the Qinling mountain range with its huge granite structure looks simple and unadorned, but its fine details make it a real paradise of fauna and flora.

In actuality, humans, in the end, also helped to create the miracle of the Qinling Mountains. From the end of the 1970s, the constant devastation of the ecological environment in the mountains has drawn the serious attention of the Chinese government and the local people. It was at that time that the Foping State Nature Reserve was established. With the giant panda as its main protective target,

▲ A leopard

▲ Wild flowers in bloom

the reserve stands at the junction of Gubei and Dongyang, demarcation lines in zoological geography. With advantageous geographic conditions and rich forest resources, it is an ideal habitat for wild animals. According to statistics there can be found over 338 species of terrestrial vertebrate animals, 34 species of state-class rare and endangered animals, and 6 species listed as state first-

▲ A takin

▲ A wild boar

class conservation animals including the giant panda.

Nearly 30,000 hectares in area, the reserve has a warm and moist climate, with 90% vegetation cover. It has very rich forest resources including 1,680 species of higher plants. Green bamboos, in particular, grow luxuriantly everywhere, providing bountiful food for giant pandas.

Taibai, the highest peak of the mountain range, is 3,736.2 meters above sea level. At an altitude of over 3,000 meters can be found ancient glacial remains of the quaternary period, which have remained intact. During even scorching hot summers, chilly winds still blow over these snowcapped mountains. In 1986, Mt Taibai was approved as a state-class nature reserve. It is located on the demarcation line between the warm temperate and subtropical zones. In terms of climate, there is a clear-cut distinction between the northern and southern slopes. A varied ecological environment is thus available for living things. Preserved in the zone is about 46,000 hectares of natural forests, with 82% vegetation cover. There are over 1,800 species of seed plants including more than 40 found exclusively in China. The Taibai red fir (Larix chinensis), in particular, grows stretching over 5,376 hectares. It is a rare tree both within and outside China.

In the reserve there are also 33 species of wild animals under the intensive conservation care of the state. The location is the northernmost distribution for giant pandas, and thus of important ecological value in the study of these animals.

On the southern slopes of the Qinling Mountains in Shaanxi's Yangxian County, there are abun-

The *B. albosinensis* forest, habitat of giant pandas

▲ Golden monkeys

dant rivers and streams. Hanjiang River and its 22 tributaries thread through this area and form extensive mountain streams and marshes. The county has over 200 ponds and numerous reservoirs. The Yangxian Crested Ibis Conservation Zone is located at an altitude of 800-1,600 meters above the southern foot of the mountains. Its valley is wide, and the majority of the ground is covered with forests— an appropriate habitat for this rare and endangered aquatic bird, the crested ibis. In the past 20 years or more, the nature reserve has given the bird a fine living environment. According to statistics from 2006, the population size of the crested ibis has increased from only 7, which were rediscovered in 2001, to over 1,000, of which the wild population has surpassed 500. Furthermore, China helped Japan to establish an artificially reproduced population of 50 birds.

By 2006, the number of nature reserves in Qiling Mountains reached 20, with a total area of several hundred thousand hectares. Among these, the Mt. Taibai zone occupies an important place in the conservation of global biodiverse species. Hence the Global Environment Facility lists the Taibai as a model conservation zone in its administrative items under China Nature Reserves.

In order to rejuvenate the entire ecological system in the Qinling Mountains, Shaanxi will continue to set up a scheduled number of new nature reserves. They will link up with the existing ones to form a much larger group. The Qinling Mountains will play an irreplaceable role in the improvement of the ecological environment in Shaanxi and the country as a whole.

Conservation Measures for Giant Pandas

Year in year out, Guan Ke bustles about in the Qinling Mountains. He is a government officer as well as a photographer. With years of experience

A charmingly naïve panda

in ecological preservation, especially in the conservation of giant pandas, he has become a unique scholar who has also gone beyond the range of research.

Since 1964, after official recognition of the distribution of giant pandas in Qinling Mountains, three comprehensive investigations have been made. The first two were completed in 1975 and 1989, and the outcome of the third was published in 2003. "Large-scale investigation has been carried out almost every 15 years. This would be inconceivable in the conservation work for any other animals," said Guan.

The result of the investigation in 2003 demonstrated that, in the Qinling Mountains the population size of the giant panda was 273, distributed within an area of about 350,000 hectares. There are also an additional 260,000 hectares for their potential habitat. The sum of the two areas is practically one tenth of the Qinling Mountains' total area.

The investigation team was composed of 51 professional members and 200 local personnel. They spent three years and encountered giant pandas 116 times in the wilds. Comparing the result with those of the earlier two investigations, a specialist has analyzed that the animal population size is increasing steadily and the area of their habitat expanding gradually. Various signs indicate that the giant pandas living in the Qinling Mountains are approaching a recovery period from their modern low point. However, due to the fact that foundational investigations have been more concentrated in the last 30 years, there was less information about the living conditions of the animal earlier than this period.

Research materials show that the giant panda population size in the Qinling Mountains dropped during the recent 1,000 years. In the past 100 years, in particular, the numbers of the animal have dropped sharply, as the environmental conditions of their habitats became worse and worse. In the 1950s, about 740,000 hectares of their habitat area remained. By the 1970s, when the first investigation was conducted, the area had dwindled to 240,000 hectares. And at the end of the 1980s, during the second investigation, giant pandas in the western section of the Qinling Mountains were disappearing one after another, as their inhabited area decreased rapidly.

Analyses and views differ in relation to the sharp reductions of panda numbers in the past 50 years. The problem of transport routes as barriers is a common argument. From 1954 to 1965, during the period when the Baocheng Railway (from

Shaanxi's Baoji to Sichuan's Chengdu) was under construction, railway builders came across giant pandas many times. Inferring from this fact, we believe that at that time the giant panda populations in the Qinling Mountains and Gansu Province must have maintained contact. After the completion of the railway, the crisscrossing tracks and the rumbling of trains ultimately separated the animals of the different locations. In the years be-

▼ Guan Ke (right), the Forestry Administration official continually patrols the Qinling Mountains.

tween 1974 and 1987, three north-south highways threading across the Qinling Mountains opened to traffic, one after the other—the state highways Nos. 108, 210 and 316—today's trunk roads in the Qinling region. Unfortunately all of them ran through the habitats of the giant pandas. In addition, in the same area at least 11 makeshift roads and other mountain paths were built in the 1970s and 1980s. In the 1980s, in particular, the reverberations from explosions in the mountains, the chugging of engines and human voices undoubtedly brought further disaster to the giant pandas.

The building of roads is vital work that is above reproach. For example, the Baocheng Railway running north and south and the express highways from Xi'an to Hanzhong in Shaanxi Province, in addition to the national highways threading across the Qinling Mountains, have rendered outstanding service in New China's economic development. However, the habitats of giant pandas in the Qinling Mountains have become fragmented due to the barriers presented by the railway and roads. In certain smaller isolated places, the limited number of giant pandas cannot but resort to mating only with others close by. This inbreeding leads to the animal gradually losing its hereditary strength and variation, as well as its evolutionary adaptability.

As a result, the population regresses, and ultimately could become extinct. The surviving ones are thus struggling hard to adapt to the new changes of their habitats.

Apart from this, there are also deep regrets for past over-felling of trees. Due to national construction needs, from the mid-1960s large-scale lumbering was conducted in the Qinling Mountains' forest zones. In the peak period there used to be over 20,000 lumberjacks working in giant panda habitats and the surrounding areas. The areas of felling amounted to nearly 630,000 hectares, equal to the total area of the giant panda habitat today. Lumbering of this kind had been carried out until 1998. "Especially in the 1980s, stimulated by the market economy, even less consideration was given to sustained forest growth and regeneration. They recklessly increased the felling according to the needs of the market. Those tall trees, together with the bamboo below them, suffered devastating sabotage. One excellent habitat after another vanished in the twinkle of an eye." Guan Ke expressed sorrow when talking about what had happened in the past century.

Giant panda conservation had started in 1964. Undergoing numerous setbacks, at the same time they achieved remarkable successes. After a num-

ber of nature reserves, especially giant panda conservation zones, grew steadily and became linked
together, a group of nature reserves in the Qinling
Mountains began to take shape. Since then, the core
part of the giant panda habitats became basically
stable. Thanks to strict conservation measures in
the nature reserves, the quality of giant panda habitats in the Qinling Mountains began to rise year by
year.

Meanwhile the disturbances caused by
highways, once the most worrisome problem, began to improve. Among them, the No. 108 state
highway is the one that runs across the core area of

the panda's habitat. For 20 years it separated Xinglong Ridge and Mt. Tianhua, the two most crucial habitats of the Qinling giant pandas. In 2000, in order to lessen the danger of traffic when giant pandas cross the Qinling Mountains in winter, a tunnel was built. The 6km-long old road that used to run over the mountains was thus abandoned. Now it is possible for giant pandas from the previously separated parts to meet each other again. Guan Ke has investigated the discarded old road atop the new tunnel. In snow-covered fields by the highway, he and his companions found obvious hoof prints of takins and other animals. "We have

▲ Takins

not yet detected traces of giant pandas as we had hoped to find, but we believe that our wish will come true in the near future," Guan said with assurance.

As for the Xi'an-Hanzhong Highway, the authorities had considered that following their initial project blueprints would mean disturbing the giant panda habitats. Before construction they specially consulted the Ministry of Forestry and adopted certain relevant proposals. Thus they came to the decision to build a tunnel at the section of the highway threading through the giant panda habitats.

In 1998, the Chinese government issued official documents to launch a natural forest preservation project in the Qinling Mountains, along with a reforestation project for cultivated lands. The latter has been particularly beneficial to the giant pandas. It has helped to bring down the cultivation line in the Qinling Mountains from 1,500 meters to about 1,350 meters. The reforested lands have become swiftly occupied with Bashan bamboo groves, giving the Qinling giant pandas more and better habitats in winter.

In 1995, the World Bank's Global Environment Facility provided funds to help the Qinling Changqing Forestry Bureau to shift its work toward the building of giant panda conservation zones. From 2001 the World Wildlife Fund (WWF), a very influential international civil organization, became concerned with the cause of giant panda conservation in the Qinling Mountains. From the very beginning this organization, using the giant panda as its logo, proposed to offer the Qinling Mountains as its 83rd "gift to the Earth." It became China's second "gift to the Earth," after its first offering, the wetlands. The Qinling Mountains have become the cynosure for all the eyes of the world concerned with the ecological environment.

Within a couple of years the WWF aided Shaanxi's Department of Forestry to construct eight giant panda conservation zones, along with five ecological greenways for the animal. An integral network has been formed for communication with the giant pandas. In 2005, WWF started its second stage of its project in the Qinling Mountains. It continued to render even more support to giant panda conservation. The project included bee-raising training for villagers, which helped to develop the local economy; rebuilding fuel-saving kitchen ranges in order to reduce pressure from firewood needs in the conservation zones; and the reformation of green vegetation in habitats, including cultivating bamboo groves, etc. The project was completed in December 2006.

The active participation of the WWF has not only brought us a lot of new thinking and concepts, but has also recommended a series of new and effective patterns in administration. Through the provision of equipped surveillance facilities in the new conservation zones and the green corridor for field petrol, assistance in drawing up administrative plans, training in professional qualifications and other activities, the WWF has helped relevant local authorities to enhance their administrative levels in conservation.

[2]

Giant Pandas: Keeping Watch
on Home for 10,000 Years

In historical documents dated back as early as 3,000 years ago can be found records relating to the giant panda. In *The Book of Songs,* China's first collection of poetry, the giant panda was called "*pixiu*" or "*xiu*" (a mythical beast). Its fur was a rare treasure, which dukes or princes offered to King Zhou. In the Western Jin Dynasty (265-316) the animal was also named "*zouyu*." Owing to the fact that the panda eats only bamboo and never harms other animals, the army designed

▲ Paddling

a logo using it on one of their flags. During a war, when one of the two confronting sides raised this flag with the panda logo, fighting would come to an abrupt stop. Moreover, according to Japan's *Annals of the Emperor's Family*, in the year of 658, Empress Wu Zetian of the Tang Dynasty offered a pair of "live white-bodied bears" (giant pandas) to Emperor Tenmu of Japan as a national gift.

The giant panda is a kind of mild and ener-vated yet stalwart animal. Their footprints once covered the whole globe during remote antiquity.

Innumerous repeated calamities occurring in global history have not eliminated them from the natural world; hence their name as "living fossil" of the glacial epoch. During the past 10,000 years, climate changes and human development have continuously encroached on the natural territory of the giant panda. The animals have had to retreat step after step. They were finally forced to live in secluded mountains and deep valleys with coniferous and broadleaf forests, at the eastern edge of the Qinghai-Tibet Plateau, at heights of 2,100 to 3,900 meters. In the past decades, due to incessant human activity, the living space for the giant pandas decreased day by day. Their habitats diminished and became limited to forests in the high mountains of Sichuan, Shaanxi and Gansu provinces.

In 2006, the Sichuan Giant Panda Nature Reserve in China was listed as a world natural heritage site. This was certainly good news, welcoming and hopeful for the giant pandas in the Qinling Mountains.

Giant Panda Subspecies in the Qinling Mountains

In 1869, after Frenchman Armand David discovered giant pandas in Sichuan's Jiajin mountainous area, his name as a biologist went down in the annals of history. However, it was not until 1964—nearly 100 years later—when scientists published their findings on the discovery of giant pandas in Qinling Mountains.

In 1932, Arthur Sowerby, a French priest, recounted this story after he had conducted a survey on Mt. Taibai. On the southern slope of the mountain a local hunter had described to him the image of a giant panda, and had even taken him to the place where its dung still remained, along with bamboo stems bitten by the animal. The priest then presumed there were giant pandas roaming the southern slopes of the Qinling Mountains. However, since there was no specimen to prove the truth of his narrative, it remained a disputed case.

In the period between 1958 and 1959, two fieldwork teams composed of teachers and students from Northwest University and Beijing Normal University found some pieces of giant panda fur and skull fragments in Chaijiaguan, Ningshan County, and Yueba, Foping County, in Shaanxi Province. After detailed study Zheng Guangmei, professor from Beijing Normal University, formally published their findings in 1964, proving that

Eating while climbing bamboo trees

there was giant panda activity in the Qinling Mountains. In the following 10 years, scientists found time and again giant panda fur and skull fragments in the same mountain range. These remains of the animal testified to the fact that there were by no means only one or two giant pandas living in the Qinling Mountains. After Sichuan, the Qinling Mountains in Shaanxi became the second giant-panda-inhabited region in China.

In the 1970s, researchers from Shaanxi Province carried out a large-scale investigation in five counties in the Qinling Mountains region. They essentially gained knowledge of the number of giant pandas and other rare animals in those counties. On January 16, 1976, when they were surveying giant pandas in the wilds, they caught a baby giant panda that had strayed from its mother. The little creature, about 10 kilograms in weight, was sent to the Xi'an Zoo, where it was given the name "Wan Wan." It became the first giant panda raised in a zoo in China.

Since December 1978, when the State Council officially approved the setting up of the Foping Nature Reserve, the Shaanxi government has built a series of natural conservation zones, namely, the Sangyuan, Motianling, Niuweihe, Qingmuchuan, Tianhuashan, Ningshan, and Guanyinshan. The number of conservation zones, with the main task of protecting giant pandas, eventually increased to 14. In April 2004, the Animal Research Institute of the Chinese Academy of Sciences and the Foping Nature Reserve jointly set up a Qinling panda field-research base in Foping's Sanguanmiao. In October of the same year, the United Nations Educational, Scientific and Cultural Organization (UNESCO) approved the Foping Nature Reserve joining the World Network of Biosphere Reserves.

In recent years, Fang Shengguo, professor of Zhejiang University, has been working together with the Foping State Nature Reserve, to compare hereditary molecular differentiation and morphology between the giant pandas in Sichuan and those in the Qinling Mountains. Professor Fang published his research findings in the US *Journal of Mammalogy,* issue No. 4, in 2005. In this authoritative journal of animal taxonomy, Fang writes: "Among the only 1,596 wild giant pandas in the world, there exists a much rarer colony–the giant panda subspecies in the Qinling Mountains. The molecular evidence indicates that, after differentiation about 10,000 years ago, the Qinling giant panda population has evolved to a subspecies. A comparison between the skull of the Sichuan subspecies and that of the Qinling one shows that the former has a big head and small teeth, but the latter has a smaller head and big teeth. The head of the Sichuan subspecies is as long as that of the bear, while the Qinling subspecies has a round head more like that of the cat. Moreover, there are obvious distinctions between the two in color. The Sichuan subspecies is deep black on its chest, white on the belly, with the lower part of the belly having white hair with black on the tips. The Qinling subspecies has a dark brown color on its chest, brown on the belly, with its lower part of the belly having white hair with brown tips. The morphological differences between the two subspecies are obvious." His observation also proved that the number of Qinling giant pandas stood at only 273. As such a valuable subspecies, their genes are more valuable than the Sichuan subspecies and they are facing a greater danger of extinction, calling for even more concern and protection.

No Rivalry with Humans

Some materials record that giant pandas have been living in the Qinling Mountains for 700,000 years. From the small-sized species that appeared in the earliest stages, they have developed to the present-day larger-size Bashi subspecies. With tenacious vitality giant pandas have been adapting to the great changes in the process of geological evolution. They have even undergone the process of the upliftment of the Qinling mountain range.

About 10,000 years ago, the Qinling giant panda had already evolved to the basic form it takes today, on a relative standing then similar to humankind. Later, the human race mastered agricultural skills and gradually exerted greater influence on the natural world. The giant panda was

▼ Eating bamboo with great relish

progressively at a competitive disadvantage.

However, there is a limit that even humankind cannot go beyond. This is the zone over 1,350 meters above sea level, where climatic conditions restrict the growth of crops. But the Qinling arrow bamboo and Mt. Bashan *mu* bamboo, the stable food for giant pandas, grow easily above that level and are even found scattered in zones with an elevation of over 3,000 meters. Hence, altitude became a natural protective barrier for Qinling giant pandas.

Giant pandas have all the characteristics of carnivorous animals, but ultimately they take bamboo as their main diet. This fact has been baffling researchers, and no one knows from what time giant pandas began to shift toward vegetarian food. However, they can be sure that stable resources of food guaranteed that the animals could make such a choice. At ground layers and on the edges of the forests or even on the wild slopes of high mountains in the Qinling Mountains, there grows everywhere luxuriant amounts of arrow bamboo, Mt. Bashan *mu* bamboo and dragonhead bamboo....

Scientists have verified that moving from being herbivore to carnivore is part of the evolutionary process of organisms. In this process the progression of the human race has accelerated the extinction of other species. Many large mammals including saber-tooth tigers have been exterminated in this competition with human beings. However, the evolution of giant pandas has proceeded in a diametrically opposite way. It is probably because of this, that they have been luckier than other contemporary living things and survived various calamities. In a sense, it is after all a judicious choice for giant pandas to take bamboo as their staple food.

In 1972, Yong Yan'ge, a 23-year-old Qinling forest ranger, was sent as a guide for the Shaanxi biological resources investigation team, composed of Chinese and foreign zoologists. From that time on, he has grown attached to the giant pandas. He worked very hard and obtained a master's degree in biology at Xihua Normal University in Nanchong, Sichuan Province. Now he has been appointed leader of the giant panda field-research base in the Qinling Mountains, and become an expert in Qinling giant panda research generally acknowledged in and outside China.

In the past decades, Yong has covered mountains and rivers, following the traces of giant pandas. He has observed and noted down many of the animals' trifling matters of everyday life, including various habits and characteristics little

▲ People carrying an injured panda
back to the protection station

known to the world.

"From April to mid-June every year, giant pandas begin to eat bamboo sprouts in Mt. Bashan *mu* bamboo groves at lower altitudes. It is the best period of the year during which they can find the most plentiful and nutritious food. In the final 10-day period of June, following the climbing temperatures, they move from lower and medium elevations to mountains over 2,200 meters above sea level to find fresh and tender bamboo sprouts in arrow bamboo groves. In August, as bamboo sprouts grow older and tougher, they change to eating tender leaves which had budded the previous year. At the end of September and the beginning of October, it begins to snow in the high mountains, with bamboo leaves curling up and turning ashy. Now giant pandas move down to eat tender leaves of the new bamboo growing in the same year, in Mt. Bashan *mu* bamboo groves below 1,900 meters above sea level. From January to March in the following year, when the frozen bamboo leaves turn tough because of the icy cold weather, they have no choice but to take green young bamboo stems as their winter food.

"Owing to limited food quality and their digestive capacity, giant pandas can store up very little fat, unlike black bears that can gather a great amount of sustenance for hibernation. In order to avoid hibernation they have to eat more, looking for food in bamboo groves even in winter blizzards. Giant pandas have rather rough hair, with a thick layer of foamed medullary substance rich in grease on the surface. The specific construction not only can keep them warm but also has the effect of dispersing wind and damp vapors. As a matter of fact,

▲ A mother panda holding her baby

living in a damp environment all the year round, giant pandas still never suffered from rheumatism. They remain undaunted in the face of winter snows and winds, eating, drinking and sleeping on snow-covered ground.

"When a panda eats bamboo leaves, it first uses its right forelimb to grasp the tip of the bamboo, then uses its incisors to bite off the leafstalk and holds it on the right corner of its mouth. Until it has collected 10 or 20 leaves, it holds on to them with its forelimbs, rolling them into the shape of a tube, which it gnaws section by section like humans eating meat rolls. In case of any snowflakes on the leaves, it would pat them off before eating.

"Occasionally giant pandas eat other species of plants, such as Chinese angelica, *Ligusticum wallichii, Cardate houttuynia*, etc. In addition to the nutrition they provide, these plants have fairly high medical value and can prevent and treat certain kinds of disease. For the purpose of gaining microelements that are indispensable for the body, pandas also lick nitrate-bearing earth from under rocky cliffs. Sometimes they even eat charcoal or bite and lick ironware or utensils stained with grease or salt sludge. On this account, some local records say pandas eat iron, and hence its name 'iron-eating creature'."

The above detailed narration of giant pandas is an excerpt from Yong's article. He discovered that, before giant pandas begin to eat Mt. Bashan *mu* bamboo stems or leaves, they first smell them and then stretch out the forelimbs to hold the bamboo stem, bite to break and pull it, and then eat the flesh. Sometimes they bend the bamboo stem to reach the leaves. Over 90% of the bamboo they choose is a year old, with young and thin skins. The lignin and cellulose inside them have an easy chewy texture, more tender and soft than that of the older bamboos. It has been attested that pandas fully depend on their sense of smell in the process of discerning food.

In the course of distinguishing new kinds of food, pandas always go by the alluring smell of the food first, rather than its form. Yong Yan'ge and some others of the same profession once tried to feed giant pandas some apples. "When we gave a whole apple to a giant panda, it smelled it first. It did so several times but could not make a decision. After we cut the apple into slices, it licked one and tasted the sweetness of the fruit. Only then did it take the slices one after the other. After that, when it saw a whole apple, it would grab it and eat it. As for eggs, potatoes or pork, they would accept these things only after we blended the food with sugar. Before that, we once tried to feed them mutton, but after smelling the meat, they became scared and ran, puffing away to one side."

The most peculiar feature of giant pandas is

their dietary habits. They live mostly on bamboo, yet still retain the simple alimentary canal of carnivores. They do not have a large appendix or a complex stomach, especially for storing food. In the alimentary canal there is no symbiotic bacteria or infusorians that can ferment the cellulose of the bamboo, to become a more absorbable nutritive substance. In fact, a giant panda can absorb no more than 20% of the carbohydrates from large quanti-

▼ Strolling through the grass

ties of bamboo it has eaten. Most of the food is excreted through the alimentary canal. For the simple reason that it can get very little nutrition from the food it has eaten, a giant panda has to spend about 14 hours chewing on bamboo stems or leaves to fill its stomach. "Quickly eat, quickly empty the bowels," is the way it copes with the problem. A 100-kilogram giant panda can consume over 50 kilograms of fresh bamboo sprouts and excrete 60 kilograms of dung every day in spring. It can eat up more than 15 kilograms of bamboo stems or leaves every day in autumn and winter.

Panda teeth are not as sharp as those of carnivores. They develop according to the needs of biting on bamboo. It has three pairs of incisors but without incising capacity. It depends on its molars to break bamboo. Unlike those of the bear species, the grinding surfaces of the molars are particularly broad and the roots are longer and stronger. In view of their whole construction, their teeth develop differently from those of carnivores. However, from the convex outline of the molars we can see that they still retain, to a certain extent, the meat-eating capacity of their ancestors. From this point of view, when pandas occasionally seize some small animals or come across corpses of other animals, they can also enjoy a delicious meal.

Sometimes, they go to nearby farmhouses to pick up discarded animal bones for a change of taste.

Reproduction is the key to survival of any animal population. For many years Yong Yan'ge has been observing giant pandas in the process of mating and reproduction. He has detailed records of the whole process.

The mating season of the giant panda is usually in spring every year from February to March, when flowers are in bloom. The bright sunshine ushers in warm and gentle winds from the northern subtropics. On tree branches by the animal paths at the convergence of valleys and mountain ridges or in narrow mountain passes, female giant pandas, using crissum fluid or urine as an estrous hormone signal, send out the peculiar smell of estrus to surrounding places. Male giant pandas would become aroused when they smell this specific odor. Observation indicates that polyandry is the mating style of giant pandas in the wild. In the process, the males always fight to decide mating priority.

Going through a 150-day pregnancy, female giant pandas enter into their parturition period in August of the same year. They in advance descend from high mountains to broadleaf forests with an elevation below 1,900 meters. Lacking particularly large tree holes in the Qinling Mountains, they usu-

▲ Looking for food in the mountains

ally look for a natural rock cave that is out of the wind and faces the sun. Then they collect some sticks as a mattress for their birthing room in the cave. In the Sanguanmiao region, over 30 rock caves suitable for giant pandas to bear their young were discovered. All of them had a southern or southeastern aspect facing the sun and out of the wind. The caves were divided into two types in terms of structure. The one referred to as the "tunnel-shaped type" has a small entrance with a deep stretching recess. This type of cave even has smaller caves interlinked one with another. Giant pandas mostly choose a smaller cave to be their birthing room. Even if it is not bright enough, the temperature inside is stable. It can also avoid any wind and rain, providing favorable conditions for the young. The other type, called a "partial rock cave" has a bigger opening, with a shallow recess. In structure, it is like an included angle formed by rock and the slope. With bad concealment factors, it has no safety guarantees. From a distance of only several meters from the entrance, one can easily see the pandas in the cave. Nevertheless, beams of sunshine can radiate straight into the cave. Giant pandas are forced to use this type of cave only when they fail to find a tunnel-shaped one. More often than not, they use it for nurturing their young one month after the birth.

In the course of raising their babies, female pandas frequently move from one cave to another. This is because, firstly, a bamboo grove around the cave can afford at most about 10 days' food for a mother panda. If the mother goes too far from the cave she would exceed a protective distance. Secondly, they might come across disturbances or potential dangers.

Stories from
China

A newly born panda is as big as a mouse, with a pink body, sparse white hair and a long tail. Only over 100 grams in weight, it cries very loudly, with its eyes still closed. One can find no correlation between its size and its voice. The crying is a signal to its mother who is out looking for food.

Within the first week after her baby is born, the mother panda sits in the cave all day long with the baby in her arms, refusing to eat and drink herself. She feeds her baby a dozen times a day, and from time to time licks the baby's belly, chest and anus, so as to stimulate and promote secretions from its sweat glands and for freer movement through its bladder and bowels. The mother panda often blocks the entrance of the cave with her back. She never lets go of her darling baby, even when

▲ The growth cycle of the baby panda

she changes her position by sitting, standing or lying down. The crook of her arms is her baby's cradle. After 20 days, when the fur has fully grown, the mother carries her baby in her mouth and takes it out of the cave to bask in the sunshine. Meanwhile the mother looks for food nearby. After 40 days, the baby opens its eyes fully, and two months later it can walk in a wobbly manner. When it is three months old it can follow its mother to move through the bamboo grove. In its 4th month, after being fed, it climbs up a tree to sleep. At sunset it produces a cry of "o ... o," to call its mother back to nurse it. This stage lasts five to six months.

When the baby is eight to nine months old, or from April to May every year, the mother panda takes it to a bamboo grove to get food. At that stage a young panda tries step by step to eat bamboo, though it still relies mainly on mother's milk. Only after it is one year old and its molars have completely grown in, does it begin to learn how to eat bamboo. In this period of time, it moves following its mother from their winter dwelling site to their summer site. In this way they can stay away from the scorching summer by staying in the higher mountains. When the weather turns cold, they will return to their winter site. A young panda is grown up at the age of one and a half years or two years, the time it begins to live independently. In case it is a female, to prevent inbreeding, it leaves for some distant parts to set up its own home there.

After investigation, it was proved that the Foping region in the Qinling Mountains is one of the concentrated habitats of wild giant pandas. There is on average one giant panda in every 2.5 square kilometers. On a slope at Huodiba near Foping's Sanguanmiao Conservation Station, Yong Yan'ge and his professional partners discovered, at the altitude of 1,400 meters in the Qinling Mountains, a giant panda reproduction base, linking one site with another. "In total, there are 12 lairs as birthing rooms linked closely together within two square kilometers. In the limits of merely 30 square kilometers, they had five new-

▲ Yong Yan'ge, a panda expert in Qinling, regards the baby panda as a child.

▲ Yong Yan'ge and his colleagues
  measuring the girth of a giant panda

borns that same year. Why is their distribution so dense?" This phenomenon has remained a mystery to Yong, the giant panda expert.

It is said that in the first 200 years after the 18th century, humans had brought the Huodiba area under large-scale cultivation. The last local inhabitant was living there until 1960. Now the region has evolved into a fine natural secondary forest with over 95% vegetation coverage. Without searching carefully, one would not find vestiges of human existence. Sanguanmiao village, closely bordering Huodiba, is the only village hidden in the remote mountains and virgin forests. In the village there are no more than a dozen households. The giant panda conservation station stands at the edge of the village. Resembling a Shangri-la, this place has no electricity and is inaccessible by traffic or mobile phone. In 2005, only after installing the first landline telephone were they finally able to communicate with the outside world. In the region of Huodiba and Sanguanmiao there are hidden traces everywhere of human activities from an earlier era. "We don't know why human beings were forced to withdraw from this place. Not long after their withdrawal, the vegetation recovered rapidly and large-sized animals including giant pandas reclaimed their habitats in the area. In view of this, Nature actually demonstrated a kind of superpower in self-regeneration," emphasized Yong.

Humans departed, and the giant pandas have returned. For hundreds of thousands of years, giant pandas have adhered faithfully to their creed, that is, no rivalry with human beings.

Giant Pandas' Human Friends

When discussing the conservation of giant pandas in the Qinling Mountains, the Xihe River should in no instance be neglected. On the map of the county region of Foping, Shaanxi Province, there is a river named Xihe flowing from the north to

▲ Xiang Bangfa (center), an ordinary villager, is a good assistant to Professor Pan in the Qinling panda research area.

the south. The Xihe Conservation Station has become the core of the Foping Giant Panda Nature Reserve, not only because it is the site where giant pandas were first discovered in this area, but also because it is a place rarely visited by human beings. Being one of the safest sites for giant pandas to live in the Qinling Mountains, it was created at great cost in terms of time and labor. The station workers have spent almost 20 lonely years in the place nearly completely cut off from the outside world.

The Foping reserve has an area of nearly 30,000 hectares, about 40% of which is part of the Xihe Conservation Station. However, based at the station are only four workers, who used to be common local farmers. The living conditions there are extremely hard. Vegetable and staple foods have to be conveyed from the village 18 kilometers away. The distance requires trekking on foot, skirting the limpid, torrential Xihe River that flows all the way by the mountain path. Since the establishment of the station in 1979, in the Xihe region they built seven surveillance routes and 18 daily patrol routes, one after another. Each of the routes is more than 25 kilometers long. In total they cover about 1, 100 kilometers trekked by the workers once every month. From the Xihe station to the Huangtongliang surveillance spot is 30 kilometers, the longest-distance route. On the way they have to cross the river 28 times. In summer the river water is breast-deep, while in winter the freezing river numbs the waders' feet. Moreover, they have to climb several precipices, including a 4km-long gorge path, half the distance of which is on top of a cliff. Any careless move means the danger of falling into the deep and swift-flowing Xihe River or hurtling down onto the stone shoals. Nevertheless, day in day out, and year after year, workers of the station keep shuttling back and forth along the routes and conducting surveys, with the giant pandas as their companions. Their efforts have resulted in a collection of basic and matter-of-fact details of the giant panda's daily life.

In the records of their daily work the workers have written the following: "In 2000, observed eight giant pandas, one of them dies a natural death; in 2001, observed 11; in 2002, 18; in 2003, 22, one dies a natural death; in 2004, 21; in 2005, 17 including two young ones, all in good health...." In the records there are also reports on takin, golden monkeys, goral, black bear, wild boar, crimson-bellied tragopan, blood pheasants, as well as other animals and plants they had found. Together with the giant pandas, the birds, animals and diverse species of plants growing over the mountains have constructed a vast expanse of land that is pure and unpolluted.

Xiong Baiquan, head of the Xihe Conservation Station, is 46 years old. In 1979, at the early stages of the Foping Nature Reserve, he came to work as an inspector and has remained at the post for 28 years. In 1981, for the first time he saw a wild giant panda walking along in a staggering fashion. From that time on, he began to love the animal. Every day in the past 28 years, in addition to taking good care of each delightful and naïve

▲ Crossing the river

giant panda, or any other wild animals passing before his eyes, he and his companions are prepared at any time to start strict struggles against poachers. In the first five years of the 1980s alone, they removed nearly 10,000 steel-wired snares set illegally for poaching wild animals in the Xihe region. On one occasion Xiong and his three companions encountered 11 poachers. Undauntedly they confronted the illegal hunters and seized eight poached musk deer.

Xiong Baiquan keeps a diary, the writing some-

times expressing his sentiments:

"Feb. 5, 2005, overcast to light snow. I went with my family from the bureau to Xihe station to celebrate Spring Festival, on duty. At six in the afternoon I saw a takin at Diaozhuangzi. Feb. 6, 2005, the 1st day of the 1st lunar month. Li Jiyu (inspector) went to carry vegetables from Dajiping village (18 km away, the nearest village to the Xihe station). Feb. 7, 2005, the 2nd day of the 1st lunar month, overcast. Went to inspect places at Xindianzi River and Xihe dam."

Xiong said that on the second day of the Spring Festival, he went with his children on an inspection duty in the mountains. "I want to let them know what their father is doing and how he gets along every day."

The diary continues: "May 6, 2004, discovered the dead body of a giant panda in Zhuhe River, 1,400 m above sea level. In the rapids, with the head of the panda pointing west... a small rock blocking the body. The hair on the parts exposed above the water surface had come off. May 8, dissected the body and discovered comminuted fractures on the left side of the animal's foreleg. Additionally, a considerable number of intestinal parasites may be another cause leading to its death. Death occurred over 10 days ago. Carried the panda's bones out of the mountains."

"March 15, 2003, first light rain, then snow with thick fog. Li Jiyu and I got lost during inspection. On the main route in a Songhua bamboo grove, 1,760 m above sea level, we came across a subspecies giant panda at a distance of less than two meters. Fished out my camera and got shots focusing on its head... Back to the station at 11:38 p.m. March 17, 2003, saw two pandas at altitude of 1,509 m... The grown-up one was keeping watch all around on a slope. I shifted my eyes to a big tree and found a young panda in it. It kept crying while its mother nearby gazed at me on the slope...."

"Oct. 30, 2003, fine to overcast. 1:30 p.m., observed a giant panda walking along the edge of a ditch, 1,500 m above sea level. From its slow movements I realized that it was ill, and in a serious condition. It moved downhill in reckless steps and stopped by a ditch, at altitude of 1,410 m. Twenty minutes' rest helped it resume its descent. At a place 10 m down, it could go no further. Back to the station at 2:10 p.m., I reported the discovery to the bureau authorities and requested rescuers."

There are further reminiscences, more sentimental, that Xiong did not record in his diary but buried deep in his heart. He said that, while waiting for the veterinarian, they, two in a group, took turns accompanying and looking after the very ill giant panda mentioned in his 2003 diary. They befriended the pitiable panda, removing lice from it, caressing it and feeding it with powdered milk. Pathetic and helpless feelings revealed in its eyes, the panda growled like a dog. The growling became louder any time they temporarily left it. Weak and ill, it was peculiarly attached to humans. It seemed as if human company was able to relieve its suffering.

The diary records a brief account of the giant panda's death: "Oct. 31, 2003… 4:30 early in the morning, a veterinarian rushed to the spot and gave the sick giant panda an injection. At 8:30 a.m., carried the giant panda back to the Xihe station; 2:50 p.m., the giant panda failed to respond to any medical treatment and died."

Presently there are still many ordinary people like Xiong Baiquan working at various giant panda conservation stations in the Qinling Mountains region. Unmindful of fame or gain they work wholeheartedly to help or look after the giant pandas, without complaints and regrets. They have become the most faithful friends of the animal. As for the local inhabitants, they take the giant panda as an auspicious animal, never doing them any harm. More often than not, they assist scientific researchers to rescue sick giant pandas or report the whereabouts of the animals. In recent years, with the purpose of giving giant pandas a more peaceful life, some farmer households have also moved out from their old homes in the conservation zone.

Academic Significance of Giant Panda Conservation in Qinling Mountains

During the time when Guan Ke, Yong Yan'ge and other Shaanxi people were diving with full enthusiasm and painstaking effort into conservation work or research on the Qinling giant panda, nearly all the domestic and foreign experts working in this field also became big supporters of the animal.

Pan Wenshi, professor of Beijing University's Biology Department and expert in giant panda research, has spent more than 10 years in the Qinling Mountains. In October 1984 Professor Pan submitted a report to the central government that expressed his disagreement with a plan scheduled to set up 13 giant panda farms in central zones of various giant panda regions across the country. He refused to accept plans for raising wild giant pandas in enclosures, insisting that the best way to conserve this type of animal is to enhance the study

▲ Professor Pan Wenshi has been working on giant panda research in the wilds of Qinling Mountains for more than 10 years.

of the wild animal populations and try every means to help them survive in more natural habitats. In November of the same year, he went for the first time into the Qinling Mountains, where some evidence roused his attention: following the rising of sea levels, the remaining sites of primeval natural landscapes there have been gradually reappearing and increasing in number; based on the same conditions, the intensity of agricultural cultivation was weakening and ultimately ebbing away at an altitude of 1,350 meters. This important phenomenon spurred Pan to decide to probe into the last chances for survival of the Qinling giant panda. He had prior research experience, for three years in the Wolong Giant Panda Nature Reserve in Sichuan Province, and had accumulated firsthand data on survival conditions of giant pandas.

In the snowy season of March 1985, Professor Pan went to the southern slopes of the Qinling Mountains, accompanied by three students including two postgraduates. On the 39th day after their arrival, 21-year-old postgraduate student Zeng Zhou fell off a precipice, giving up his life on a journey to look for giant pandas. Three months later, of the research group begun through such ill-fated circumstances, only two members remained—the professor himself and a female postgraduate who had just celebrated her 20th birthday.

From 1984 to 1999, a total of 15 postgraduates participated in the research work. Those 15 years had elapsed in a flash. For all that time Professor Pan never stood for any loafing. When he thinks about how his youthful group demonstrated the high spirits of unity and radical fervor in the face of natural obstacles as well as trials and tribulations of the human world, subtle emotions, solemn yet stirring, rise from the bottom of his heart.

Professor Pan, recalling those unforgettable days and nights, remembers how owing to a shortage of research funds, they had to plan everything painstakingly. The postgraduates never booked sleepers for the 35-hour train trip from Beijing to Hanzhong, nor stayed overnight anywhere en route. After that long train ride, they had to take an 8-hour long-distance bus, and then wait for rides on trucks conveying logs from the forests, before they could finally reach their field station. All the males were required to take up the heaviest work. After their daily work in the fields, on the way back to the campsite, every one of them had to carry a log of waste timber for fuel, no matter how fatigued they were. To cut back on expenses they generally did not hire local workers as assistants, but did the kitchen and household chores themselves, such as chopping firewood and cooking.

Giant pandas live in mountainous areas at elevations of 2,000 to 3,000 meters. The winter season in the Qinling Mountains has freezing temperatures. With the aim of tracking giant pandas, Professor Pan and his group usually stayed in the mountains during the winter. One year he spent the Spring Festival in the mountains with a postgraduate student. To save time and charcoal, they boiled potatoes and rice together in a large pot, to serve as their meals over several days. Not until they moved to a new workplace, would they boil another pot.

Professor Pan continued: "Working conditions in the wilds were very hard. Looking back, I felt one of the hardest things was the lack of meat dishes. Sometimes, we even did not have enough staple foods, and felt hungry almost all the time. These conditions lasted eight years. During that period, during bitterly cold nights we stayed in old rundown wooden work-sheds, unable to keep out the wind blowing from all sides. We dared not make a fire. All we could do was wrap our bodies into down sleeping bags. With one hand holding a candle, using the other we wrote out our research records. When we got up early the following morning, we'd find the water in the basin had frozen into a big lump of ice."

In August 1989, "Jiao Jiao," the first female giant panda to wear a radio-tracking neck-ring, gave birth for the first time. Pan Wenshi and his students began to track the mother and baby panda every day around the clock, studying their activities until the baby was five months old. In the autumn of 1994, they installed a small closed-circuit surveillance system in Jiao Jiao's birthing room in a cave. From the first day Jiao Jiao gave birth to a third cub, every four days they recorded the activities of the mother panda and her baby for three days and nights. "We stayed in another cave 50 meters from Jiao Jiao's cave. We recorded all their voices and activities until the young panda was five months old and they began their new life in the woods." In his plain fashion Professor Pan narrated his experiences in the wilds.

In 1988, Pan and his group detected in the Qinling Mountains a 1,670 sq. km area that was possibly one of the last habitats of giant pandas. In 1992, they came to the conclusion that Qinling giant pandas had normal reproductive capacity. All the females wearing the radio-tracking neck-rings had given birth to babies. This indicated that the Qinling giant panda is a hopeful population that can continue to survive and procreate. However, in 1993 Pan noticed that there was no sign of improvement in the circumstances for the Qinling giant panda compared with those of eight years ago. Giant pandas were facing increasing dangers due to the reckless lumbering spreading to the last primeval larch forest on the main ridge of the Qinling Mountains over 2,800 meters above sea level. This forest had gradually formed after the end of the last glacial period, 12,000 years ago, and is now still in its growth period. Confronted with this extreme situation—giant pandas would lose their last natural sanctuary on the desolate southern slopes of the Qinling Mountains—Professor Pan started to appeal to all the authorities concerned to reduce the amount of timber being cut, so as to give the giant panda one last chance for survival.

From 1993 to 1994 saw the continuous submission of reports to the central government by Pan, until it brought to an end all the tree-felling on the 300-sq. km forest zone on the southern slopes of the Qinling Mountains.

 A brown panda and a black panda mating

In the spring of 1999, five years after the halt to the clear-cutting, Professor Pan returned to the research site in the Qinling Mountains. Before his eyes there were scenes of luxuriant vegetation. The highways for timber transport used in those years had been replaced by grass and plants. The surveillance system revealed 15-year-old Jiao Jiao taking her fifth child out of the deep valley. The other four young—two male and two female ones, with their descendants, also lived in the bamboo grove nearby. "Does it mean that the Qinling giant pandas have possibly made it through the very long night of 12,000 years, in an evolutionary history that began before agricultural civilization? Is it possible that they are ushering in a new dawn permitting them to rejuvenate and multiply?" Professor Pan put forward wishful hopes from an academic perspective, based on the results achieved through his 15 arduous years of research work in the wilds.

Pan Wenshi and Professor Hu Jinchu are two symbols in the domain of giant panda research in China. Now advanced in age, Hu Jinchu is an expert in giant panda research who enjoys an international reputation. Many of his students have become pillars in this field.

In 1957, Hu Jinchu received a master's degree in vertebrate science from Beijing Normal

University. The turning point in his life really occurred in 1974. That same year the state decided to conduct investigations on resources for the giant panda and other rare animals in Shaanxi, Gansu and Sichuan provinces. Hu was invited personally to take charge of the investigation in Sichuan. From that time on, he has spent half his lifetime on giant panda research. For several decades, Hu has been shuttling between mountains and rivers in Sichuan. With his students he has promoted the subject of Sichuan giant panda research to the international forefront. Not only did he open up the Wolong Giant Panda Nature Reserve, but he also continuously sent a range of research personnel to take part in the work of giant panda conservation and procreation. Thanks to his unremitting efforts, Wolong has long remained the landmark of giant panda survival and reproduction in China. That is why Hu has become the chief expert on pandas in the Animal Research Institute of the Chinese Academy of Sciences.

The Wolong Nature Reserve has successfully raised over 80 giant pandas in enclosures, the largest panda population bred by humans in the world. However, Hu Jinchu holds the same viewpoint as Pan Wenshi. He said, in relation to the conservation and reproduction of the giant panda, it is not

▲ Professor Hu Jinchu, known as "the master of the giant panda research area"

his wish to raise the animal in enclosures. In captivity, only one tenth of the males are able to mate, and no more than one third of the females can bear young. Moreover, as time passes, giant pandas bred in captivity tend to completely lose their procreative capacity after 50 years. The artificially raised giant pandas in the Beijing Zoo and Chengdu Zoo give evidence in support of this perspective. In contrast, in the wilds of both Sichuan and Shaanxi, twins have been found, alive and active in certain giant panda families. They also found several male giant pandas fighting for mating rights. All this indicates that hopes for giant panda conservation and reproduction lies in the wilds, in mountain forests vibrant with life.

Professor Hu believes that the Qinling Mountains is the region in which China's giant pandas are distributed with highest density. This is due to continuous human encroachment. It is of great significance in the research on the present living environment of Qinling giant pandas. Living in secondary forests close to human beings, they are not shy of people. In recent years, thanks to effective human efforts, the living environment of the animals has taken a turn for the better, though new problems are emerging. For example, since reforestation, the blindly imported Japanese larch was widely sown in some regions. It has greatly threatened the habitats of giant pandas. When grown in forests this big-crown species of tree will shade other plants under it from sunshine. Unable to absorb nutrition and moisture, the lower vegetation will gradually die out. In addition, larch itself has great reproductive capacity. The seeds of it can spread rapidly in various ways, and seriously damage the biological and genetic diversity of the environment around it. By now, Japanese larch has

About 10,000 years ago, the Qinling giant panda had already evolved to the basic form it takes today.

grown into forests in some sections of the Qinling Mountains. The trees are eating away the corridors leading to giant panda populations. In the past, lumbering and highway construction, along with other human activities, separated the habitats of giant pandas, and now the larch has become a new barrier.

If we can properly solve the problem of giant panda habitat protection and make a plan to cultivate appropriate species of trees on reforested lands, so as to build corridors for giant pandas, we could certainly help to further promote the work of giant panda conservation and reproduction. It is a cause of practical significance that could also be used for reference in other places.

George B. Schaller, a US professor, is a foremost distinguished contemporary zoologist. He has headed many international research programs. From 1980 to 1985, he took part in the "Panda Plan," organized by the World Wildlife Fund, making several visits to study giant pandas deep in the Wolong Mountains in Sichuan. He worked side by side with Hu Jinchu at the Wolong Ecological Observation Station and introduced Chinese experts to the latest scientific ideas and technologies. In 1992, based on his experiences in China, he wrote and published a book entitled *The Last Panda*, which caused a great sensation in the United States. In December that same year, at Pan Wenshi's invitation, Schaller visited a research zone located in the Qinling Mountains. He saw three giant pandas at a short distance in the Changqing area. One of them was only a delightful tiny downy ball, sleeping peacefully in a bamboo grove.

Schaller was greatly moved by and admired his Chinese colleagues' passion for their work including their research. In his book he narrated what he had learned about Hu Jinchu, Pan Wenshi and Yong Yan'ge. He regarded Hu Jinchu as an outstanding naturalist, who had passed on to him a lot of knowledge about birds and forest biology. Schaller said it was a pleasure to do field work with Hu, because Hu was happy in his work no matter how foul the weather was or how rough and uneven the paths ahead. He had a venturesome spirit and was full of curiosity. Pan Wenshi had conducted all types of laboratory research. Schaller said he had first underestimated Pan's interest in pandas. Pan later took charge of China's best research plan on pandas, not in Wolong, but in the Qinling Mountains in Shaanxi. On mentioning Yong Yan'ge, Schaller said that he was very impressed by his study of pandas in Foping. Yong had told Schaller that in 48 hours the panda drank water five times and ate 14 meals, each time from one and a half to five hours. Electronic tracking devices could not obtain such detailed data. Schaller said that he hoped he could find young biologists as dedicated as Yong Yan'ge for his plan.

Up to now, George Schaller still bustles about in his work on China's giant panda, as well as on the conservation of other wild animals on the verge of extinction. He says we know what giant pandas need. They need a forest with growing bamboo, a cave where they can bear their young, and freedom to move about without interference. He said this after he conducted his research work for some time jointly with Chinese scientists on wild giant pandas in the Qinling Mountains. He provided further academic weight to the research on the giant panda's survival in the Qinling Mountains.

[3]

Crested Ibises: Out of Danger of Extinction

In 1981, after Japan had already announced to the world that the wild crested ibis had become extinct, Chinese scientists discovered seven of the species living in a secluded spot in the Qinling Mountains in Yangxian County, southern Shaanxi Province. Today, after 26 years the population size of the endangered bird has sprung from seven to over 900. It cannot be said that they have finally survived their doom, but there is hope ahead. This is because Chinese scientists and the Yangxian people, hand in hand, have been carrying on their

▲ A crested ibis spreading its wings

work on the conservation and reproduction of crested ibis. Their success can serve as a model in the history of human rescue of endangered species and, moreover, their work has never ceased.

"Gem of the East" and Divine Bird

Fossilized ibis, discovered in oil shale from archeological excavations, testify that in the Eocene epoch 60 million years ago there were already ibises in existence. In ancient times, crested ibises were more widely found. A century ago they began to appear only in China, Japan, Korea and Russia, and become a specialty bird species of eastern Asia. Since the 1930s, following the worsening ecological environment, the population size of the bird has sharply dwindled, their distribution area having diminished rapidly. Crested ibis is a favorite bird of the Japanese people. In 1957, when the numbers of the bird were found to be drastically reduced, the Japanese government listed the crested ibis as a "special natural emblem." At the 12th conference of the International Council for Bird Preservation, held in Tokyo in 1960, the crested ibis was declared as an "international priority bird to preserve." At the end of the 1970s the bird disappeared from Russia and the Korean Peninsula. Japan captured the remaining four crested ibises and raised them artificially, together with another one kept individually in cage. They tried to induce them to procreate, but their efforts were ultimately in vain. Crested ibis, known as the "gem of the East," became one of the most treasured as well as most endangered species in the world.

A passage in *Enlightened Compendium of Materia Medica*, edited in Japan in the 19th century, described: "... Looks like the egret in appearance, it has long hair on the crest, an ashy back, ruddy inner side feathers with scarlet plume stems. Viewed from the ground, the flying birds look vibrant with their enchanting colors. Their feathers can be used for arrow making. Able to fly long distances, they usually nest in remote forests... They are very noisy when they cry in flocks, sounding raucous like crows but deeper...." In China, the crested ibis is also named "red egret" or "red crane," a species of medium-sized aquatic wildfowl, about 80 centimeters in length, 1,600-2,000 grams in weight. They have long curved beaks, scarlet beak tips, legs and claws, and drooping willow-leaf-shaped feathers on the back of their necks. In spring, their plumage turns lead-gray, in summer, autumn and winter changing into white. The wing feathers become pink in bright sunshine, as sparkling and crystal-clear as precious gems.

In 1852, German scholars first set up a new genus of bird named "Nipponia," with the crested ibis listed under it. In 1920, the crested ibis was universally given a standardized name, that is, *Nipponia nippon*. According to related materials, the crested ibis belongs to long-lifespan birds, able to survive as long as 30 to 40 years. The mature birds have reproductive capacity by the age of two.

The *China Red Data Book of Endangered Animals: Aves*, compiled by the World Conservation Union (or IUCN), writes to the effect that crested ibises, resident birds, fly leisurely in flocks for short journeys to low mountains or plains in autumn and winter. From April to May they begin to make nests, laying two to four eggs per brood each year. The eggs are light green with fine brown spots. The parent birds incubate the eggs by turns and breed the young. After around 30 days the young birds break the shells, and after about 40 days of maturing they leave the nest.

Crested ibises, when flying in the air, look free and elegant; and graceful and poised when walking on the ground. At rest they usually stick their beaks into the feathers at their backs, allowing their beautiful crest feathers to dance in the breeze. Guan Ke described his first sight of ibises found by a stream in a forest in the Qinling Mountains. He expressed his feelings in the following way: "When I saw them soaring freely between the azure sky dotted with white clouds and the blue waters of the stream, I was intoxicated by the hues of white tinged with red, as resplendent as rosy clouds hidden in the inner sides of their wings. With great admiration, I felt as if I were looking on a type of noble temperament I had never before sensed. I was surprised to find such a rarity in the world. No wonder there are so many people who regard

Flying

crested ibises as divine birds."

Korean and Japanese poets have expressed their grief over the endangered crested ibis. A Korean folk rhyme describes the crested ibis:

> *"They are the birds perhaps seen perhaps not,*
>
> *Yet cannot be, tao-ki tao-ki, their woeful cries.*
>
> *Where do you go? To see your mothers? Where suns rise? "*

A Japanese poet also revealed his sorrowful feelings:

> *"In Niutou* Forest, enwrapped in soft dawn light,*
>
> *Breezes echo the crowing chorus of crested ibises.*
>
> *Carefree coasting the celestial river, gilded in morning glow.*
>
> *Oh, where will this flock of crested ibises soar tomorrow?*
>
> *Wisps off burning coal float on the winds and dust the mountains.*
>
> *The haunts of crested ibises will exist no more tomorrow,*
>
> *Silhouettes of crested ibises fade from dells and open airs by Guojian. "*

*Ox Head

From ancient Chinese poets' descriptions related to crested ibises, it seems that the birds have always been seen as a vibrant life form. The verses in an ancient poem depict: "They frolic on the jade water in the wind,/Alight on the dyke in golden sunshine." The poet seems to compare the crested ibises to graceful beauties. There is another depiction in an ancient verse: "Crested ibises romp amidst duckweed and algae,/wandering in winding streams." This seems to indicate to people of today that, at one time crested ibises could be found throughout mountain streams or any places with running water.

> "Crested ibises whirl down with grace to swim
>
> In the pools of spring, or rest in green woods.
>
> Their feathers like scissors midst a riot of dyes.
>
> Swirling to land from long flights, they fold their wings.
>
> Eluding men they lead their young to remote chasms.
>
> As they glide through water, ripples glisten, spread in all circles."

This provides an enchanting vision of crested ibises by the riverside, as expressed in a verse by the Tang dynasty poet Zhang Ji. Nowadays, similar scenes can often be found around Yangxian County in Shaanxi's Hanzhong area.

Yaojiagou—Where Crested Ibises Were Rediscovered

At the end of the 1970s, Japanese people, looking to find crested ibises, placed their hopes on China's mainland. They believed that only in the wide expanses of land in China could sites be found for any surviving crested ibises. But for over 20 years there had been no news of any crested ibises in China. Then the painstaking task of looking for the crested ibis was assigned to Liu Yinzeng and others in the Animal Research Institute of the Chinese Academy of Sciences. In the following three years, the scientists' footprints covered over half the country. However, with the exception of old evidence in some places in which crested ibises once lived, they found no signs of the birds.

In 1981, Liu Yinzeng and his investigation group came to Shaanxi's Yangxian County on the southern slopes of the Qinling Mountains. A villager told them that, near his home he had seen big birds locally referred to as "red cranes." The next day, led by the villager, the group arrived at Jinjiahe in Yangxian at dusk, after a long arduous journey. Just as they were mounting a mountain ridge, they heard the queer crying of a bird overhead. Liu raised his head and sighted a crested ibis, like in his dreams, flying slowly past. Overcome with exhilaration, he lost his footing. When he found his feet again, the bird was nowhere to be seen.

They were having a rest in the villager's house when suddenly they again heard the memorable cry coming from a large tree behind the house. They rushed to the place and, sure enough, found a crested ibis nest, in which sat two adult birds. Their joy over the discovery knew no bounds. The following day in Yaojiagou they discovered another crested ibis nest with two adult birds and three newborns. Among the last population of wild crested ibis, there in Yangxian County, they finally confirmed seven crested ibises in total, four adult birds and three young ones. Liu said afterward: "It had been like looking for a needle in a haystack, only glimmers of hope from the beginning of my long quest for the crested ibis. In three years, I covered nearly 50,000 kilometers from Hunan Province in the north to Guangdong in the south, Gansu in the west and the coastal provinces in the east. My journey followed the historical distribution of crested ibises over 12 provinces. I had a crystal-

A golden bush robin

A large cuckoo

A daurian redstart

A blood pheasant

Birds that co-exist
with the crested ibis

clear objective, being, I should go through all the places with natural environments suitable for the survival of crested ibises. Then I could give an explicit and credible answer to academic circles studying birds. To the end of my days I shall never forget my journey to Yangxian and what we discovered at Yaojiagou."

Yaojiagou is an out-of-the-way small mountain village, located 1,200 meters above sea level on the southern slopes of the Qinling Mountains. It is named after a canyon of the same name. The 5km-long canyon runs northwest by east. A brook flowing from the depths of the canyon empties itself into the Youshui River. In winter, in the paddy fields on both sides of the brook grow diverse species of plants. A mere seven households live scattered in the village. Sparsely populated, the village has maintained a semi-primitive state in its natural environment, with 80% forest cover. Secondary deciduous broadleaf forests, mixed with shrubbery, form the vegetation. It is a place where oak, lacquer, poplar, Chinese pine, willow, wild walnut, Manchurian ash, wild cherry and other trees all grow healthily. Under the trees are found wild shrubs such as wild Chinese prickly ash, kiwi fruit, and so on. In the woods, many birds, including magpies, crows, rufous-headed crowtits, thrushes, white-throated laughing thrushes, lesser owls, white-fronted tits, green barbets, spotted doves, golden pheasants, reeve's pheasants and ring-necked pheasants, build their nests. Wildlife such as tufted deer, musk deer, serow, wild boars and black bears live deep in the forest. In this area where many crested ibises once built nests are found 15 centuries-old Qinggang trees over 20 meters high from root to crown. Climbing across the mountain ridge exactly opposite the nesting zone, they found winter paddy fields stretching as far as the horizon. It is due to such a superb natural environment that the crested ibises had chosen Yaojiagou as their secluded abode.

The original records of the crested ibis conservation zone in Yangxian County provide a detailed story of Yaojiagou and its crested ibises:

"On May 27, 1981, at Yaojiagou of the Baliguan Commune they found a brood of six young ibises including one dead, and one fallen on the ground. At that time Liu Yinzeng was responsible for breeding of the birds. The five birds and the two others discovered in Jinjiahe were labeled 'Qinling No. 1 Crested Ibis Population.' On June 23, with the approval of the PRC Ministry of Forestry, the male young bird that had fallen from the nest in Yaojiagou was named 'Hua Hua' and taken to the

▲ Taking a rest on a tree

Beijing Zoo by Wang Decheng. In July, a temporary crested ibis conservation group was formed by the Forestry Bureau in Yangxian, stationed at Yaojiagou to carry on professional conservation observation.

"On September 11, 1983, one young bird fell sick after being fed and released in Yaojiagou, and died on the 13th, after 116 days of existence. The cause of its illness is still unknown. In December, in Yaojiagou we built two 12-cubic-meters cement breeding ponds to raise loaches as food for crested ibises.

"In August 1984, three houses and two kitchens were built for observation sites in Yaojiagou. In September, the crested ibis station invested RMB 1,500 for the establishment of the Yaojiagou Crested Ibis Primary School. There were six students, given lessons by Zhao Zhihou, a contract worker from one observation site."

......

During those days Yaojiagou was brimming over with joy and laughter. The whole world was sharing in the happiness of the rediscovery of the crested ibis. However, on a sorrowful day in September 1990, one of the members of the crested ibis family was killed in Yaojiagou, as it was flying through the skies. After that time, no crested ibis ever returned to the nest in the village. Later, according to a villager, in the middle of March every year, from 1991 on, the crested ibis that had lost its other half, always comes back to the village. In the afternoon it flies overhead, toward the setting sun. The evening glow dyes its pink wings with golden hues. It cries loudly as it circles in the air. Then it drops onto a tree, and once settled it folds the wings quietly and gazes around. Even as night falls, the bird still perches by itself on a branch, oblivious to the surrounding darkness that gradually swallows it up. It stays there until the forest welcomes the first rays of sun. It then usually unfolds its beautiful wings at 8:00 or 9:00 in the morning, and then reluctantly leaves the village, for a faraway place.

Through this sad and moving story, the villagers pour out their emotions of remorse and express their longing for their beloved birds.

Crested Ibis Conservation through Law

In the criminal archives of the Yangxian judicial department can be found this verdict written in detail: "On September 12-14, 1990, at the Leicaogou Reservoir in Laomiao village, in Yangxian's Wujian township, successive cases of an exceptionally vicious crime took place. Three crested ibises were killed... The two criminals in the cases, Pi Peihai and Xiang Bokai, were apprehended and brought to justice. They were sentenced to seven and five years' imprisonment, respectively." One of the three crested ibises killed was from Yaojiagou. The tragedy has led to two consequences: firstly, the crested ibises never returned to nest in Yaojiagou; secondly, the judgments of the cases brought about the confiscation of hunting rifles in the entire county of Yangxian, in order to put an end to all such tragedies.

Since the discovery of crested ibises in Yangxian in 1981, the conservation work in the county has been carried out according to law. In a series of official papers or laws and regulations issued one after another, there are detailed articles that make clear: No hunting in crested ibis habitat zones. No lumbering in forests in which crested ibises live. Pesticides and chemical fertilizers are forbidden to be used in paddy fields. No new reclamation areas within a circumference of 300 meters from any nest zones of crested ibis. All the cultivated land should maintain their current status. No reclamation in cases where land lies fallow in turn, etc. To varying extents such initial conservation

▼ Looking for food in the river

measures have played a leading role.

In the past 26 years, six criminals involved in three cases of killing crested ibis in Yangxian have been persecuted for criminal liability. This has made a tremendous impact and seriously frightened off potential criminals in Yangxian and beyond. At the same time, at highway crossings the relevant authorities have set up signs detailing laws and regulations for the conservation of crested ibises. Likewise, eye-catching slogans can also be seen on high buildings. Educational information, including films related to crested ibis conservation or TV specials, are broadcast regularly. All this has made a deep impression on every one of the Yangxian people as well as all visitors to the county.

The Yangxian Crested Ibis Rescue and Breeding Center, with an area of 1.5 hectares, is located three kilometers to the north of the city of Yangxian. It is currently the only center in China integrating scientific research, teaching and conservation. It houses 30 breeding cages, within 1,000 square meters, a hall for crested ibis public education and teaching that combines films, TV, photographs, specimens and ecological simulation, into an organic whole; and a crested ibis releasing shed, 35 meters high and 8,000 square meters in area. Caoba village, near the center, is a night-perching ground

▼ Crested ibis practice monogamy. The female ibis and the male ibis spend their lives together, and never separate from each other, till death do they part.

▲ Crested ibises are very beautiful, their bodies all white, except for pink wings and scarlet heads. They are listed as one of the top five rarest birds on earth.

for crested ibises. Every night over 60 crested ibises and 1,000 other co-existing birds stay overnight there. In spring every year, students from primary schools and secondary schools in Yangxian visit the center and the wild crested ibis habitat, in the process of conducting investigations, so as to improve their understanding and arouse their enthusiasm for the rare bird.

The Yangxian Conservation and Observation Station has become a core for public education and conservation work. For many years, workers at the station have been tracking the activities of the crested ibises and striving to protect them. Overall they follow the birds closely wherever they go. In order to allow the birds to have more and better nests in high and cold mountains, they provide saplings to the villagers and encourage them to plant trees on fallow lands, even covering any expenses of tree planting. The administrative rights and ownership of such planting belongs to the owners of the land. The species of trees they have chosen are also those preferred by the local people, such as China fir, eucommia, official magnolia, among others. All this has greatly aroused the enthusiasm of the masses for crested ibis conservation. Starting from 1985, the station has announced that those who give information on the whereabouts of crested ibises, including the discovery of nesting sites or any dead bodies of birds, their new activity sites, and of sick or wounded birds, will receive a suitable reward. Consequently, people from different villages have provided a total of 230 items of information about the crested ibis, including 87 nest findings and over 50 sick or wounded birds. They have also played an important role in the effective surveillance of the bird's population size.

The migrating season, once every year, is the time when the crested ibis population travels in large flocks, after the end of the breeding season. In this period the birds have a large appetite and a wide sphere of activities. At the same time it is also the period that poses the greatest potential threat from their natural enemies or human beings. In addition to large-group migration, the birds also tend to move about in smaller flocks or even individually. The young birds that leave the nest that same year are still too weak to adapt to the natural environment, or to resist disease or natural enemies, and hence the work of surveillance and conservation becomes even more difficult. In view of this situation, the Yangxian authorities have demarcated the crested ibis night-perching ground as a special conservation site, as well as requisitioned big trees with crested ibis nests in some parts of

▲ Popularizing wild animal protection knowledge among students

the region. Tree-felling is strictly forbidden within these areas. The trees for night-perching are marked with standardized numbers, with adhered signs, and kept on file. Conservation signs have also been put up in essential sections or areas such as rivers, ponds, reservoirs or natural wetlands where crested ibises gather to look for food. Goose or duck breeding and fishing are strictly forbidden in the above-mentioned waters. To avoid harm towards crested ibises, no baits can be laid for other aquatic fowls, and no hunting is allowed in these areas. The rules have effectively guaranteed a settled life and reproductive process for the birds.

Through 20 years of meticulous care in conservation, wild crested ibis habitats have expanded from the first site in Yangxian to seven counties or regions under the administration of Shaanxi's Hanzhong city. The activity area of the birds covers over 3,000 square kilometers. Now Yangxian County remains the distribution center and main breeding site that accounts for 98% of the wild crested ibises in the area.

Divine Birds Keeping Company with Humans

How have crested ibises been able to survive only in Yangxian, while they have vanished in wider areas? According to the analysis of scientists, this is mainly due to its relatively slow economic development, so that pesticides and chemical fertilizers are seldom used in the county. Traditional ways of cultivation, including lands left to lie fallow in turn, have been maintained. Large expanse of winter paddy fields left idle from the previous year's season provide crested ibises with essential guarantees for survival. Moreover, local villagers regard the crested ibis as a divine bird. Very few people would hurt them. It is also one of the important reasons why crested ibises have been able to survive in this place.

Years of experience in field investigation testify to the fact that living conditions that crested ibises depend on must include human households, big trees and paddy fields. The three factors are interlinked, each closely with each other; none of the three is dispensable. Crested ibises are shy of humans by nature but, at the same time, they also cannot live without people. They tend to live hidden in mountain streams in forests but close to farmhouses. In the daytime they catch loaches, insects, frogs, crab, fish or shrimp in paddy fields, streams or brooks. They make greater demands on their living surroundings than other birds do. They prefer habitats covered mainly with deciduous broadleaf or evergreen broadleaf forest, because the high and large crowns are beneficial for them to build nests. They look for food only in unpolluted paddy fields or clean streams. Of eccentric yet quiet disposition and afraid of loud noises, they usually venture out in pairs or in small groups.

Caihe village is situated 10 kilometers away from Yangxian's Huaishu town, on the southern slopes of the Qinling Mountains to the north and on the northern banks of the Hanjiang River to the south; nearby are many lakes and wetlands with dense pine groves all around. With plentiful food in winter, it is a favorable habitat for crested ibises. In the mid-spring of 1998, the first pair of crested ibis appeared unexpectedly in a pine grove near the village. In early spring of 2002, the crested ibises stealthily built their first cozy nest in a pine tree behind villager Cai Daosheng's house. In the same year, three young birds were hatched. Cai reported the case immediately to the crested ibis conservation station in Yangxian. Workers from the station took protective actions and began to periodically check the young birds' health and measure their length and weight. Ultimately two of them survived. In the depths of winter, 2002, some more crested ibises suddenly came to the village. In 2003 they found one more new nest. In 2004, the birds mounted to over 30. In the winter of 2005, the number began to increase greatly. At present Caihe village has become the largest night-perching ground and breeding zone for wild crested ibises. In a small ravine, one kilometer long and 400 meters wide, eight nests hold about 80 crested ibises in spring, and as many as 172 during autumn.

Living with crested ibises harmoniously, the Caihe people have demonstrated meticulous care for the birds. The Chinese pine grove 20 meters behind the backyard of Li Peizhen, a teacher from the Caihe Primary School, is one of the important sites where crested ibises stay overnight. Talking about crested ibises, he becomes very excited. He says the birds have stayed there for four years since the first pair arrived in 1998. From then on his family neither cut firewood nor do they even collect falling sprigs in the forest. Li knows the habits of the birds very well. For example, the birds begin to sing at 5:00 in the morning and start to look for food at 6:20. They return in groups of three or five at 6:40 in the evening. Once the teacher discovered a young bird, who had been left alone in the nest, that tried to take wing but instead had fallen on the ground. He and his son immediately carried the bird in a bamboo basket and carefully put it back into the nest with the help of a wooden ladder.

On a Chinese pine 25 meters behind the house of elderly Cai Daosheng, there is a crested ibis' nest built by the first pair of the birds seen in Caihe village. By now over 60 crested ibises have been hatched in the nest. The elder became the first villager the conservation station appointed as a crested ibis attendant. Around the clock he carries out his duties with his son by turns, allowing no strangers or draught animals to approach the forest. He even stopped keeping dogs at home, for fear that barking would disturb the birds. From March 1 to June 1 every year, the breeding season of the crested ibis, is the busiest time for the family. They spread a net under the tree in case the newborn birds fall down from the tree, and wrap the tree trunks with plastic sheets to prevent snakes from crawling up. Not until they find the young birds leaving the nest to look for their own food, does the family finally breathe a sigh of relief.

Every spring, when the Caihe villagers go out to plant seedlings in the paddy fields, is the season when crested ibises and humans find each other at the shortest distances. The birds look for loaches or eels, following on villagers' heels. When people turn over the soil to plant potatoes, the birds would trail closely behind looking for insects in the up-turned soil. If you toss them an earthworm, they would fly over to the spot, sometimes even less than one meter from where you are standing.

In Caihe village no one, old or young, has chased after or scared the crested ibises. The birds, in turn, treat people as their old friends. They often perch still on the ridges of villagers' houses or trees in front of their homes, gazing quietly and genially at people. With the aim of providing a more favor-able living environment for the birds, the Caihe people grow green paddy without ever spraying pesticides in their fields. In winter, they leave a special stretch of paddy fields for the birds to look for food in. They also develop loach breeding and storage, or raise other favorite foods of the birds.

The pupils of Caihe Primary School have be-come a new generation of crested ibis assistants. They put forward the following slogan: "Love the mountains, love the rivers and love the birds." They write on blackboards on campus: "Attention, all teachers and students, please tell your family mem-bers and neighbors not to set off firecrackers on festive occasions, because crested ibises, our sisters, live with us." Over recent years the pupils' proposal has resulted in no firecrackers being let off on any festivals, for fear that they would scare off their beloved birds.

Rescuing Crested Ibises from Extinction

China has a 2,000-year history in the breeding of crested ibises. In *Records of the Historian*, written by Sima Qian, a passage describes birds being raised in the imperial garden or hunting grounds of the Han Dynasty (206 BC - AD 24). Among them is the crested ibis: "The emperor was wandering in the imperial hunting ground…swans, bustards, geese and ibises glided on the water." After the re-emergence of the crested ibis in 1981, scientists started experimenting in artificial breeding. Of the present crested ibis population in China, almost half the number was bred by humans.

In 1983 Professor Liu Yinzeng took charge of the experiment in crested ibis artificial breeding at Yaojiagou. An original file from the Yangxian Crested Ibis Natural Conservation Zone records: "In June 1983, in Yaojiagou three young birds fought vigorously for food. At noon on the 15th, the attendant, braving the rain, took two of the birds down from the nest. After 75 days' artificial breeding, he released them."

On March 8, 2007, staff from the Rare Wildlife Rescue and Breeding Research Center, in Shaanxi Province, set free 10 pairs of artificially bred crested ibises, in order to complete an experiment on releasing them back into the wilderness.

The incident happened during the rainy season, when food was lacking. In comparison with other normal birds with the same lifespan, the 30-day-old crested ibises in the nest were three fourths their size. At the observation spot in Yaojiagou, the scientific researchers in a spacious field set up a breeding shed, facing the sun and about 60 meters away from the tree with the nest. In the shed they set up branches where the young birds could rest or exercise their wings, and provided them with water and loaches. At first the young birds were quite frightened of people. They hid themselves nervously in a corner at the back of the shed, looking around edgily, then standing still, shivering, and lying on the ground or excreting. Two days later, after realizing that the humans meant them no harm, they began to approach the breeders and cry out for food. Four days later they began to eat the loaches on the hands of the breeders. Ten days later they had the same good appetite just as those young birds outside the shed. They poked their long beak into the pail to gulp down the loaches. If they felt hungry but couldn't find food near them, they would approach the breeders and cried for food. Sometimes, female birds, flying back to feed their young in the nests, happened to hear the crying. They would turn back and feed the birds behind the railing of the shed. It was an extra meal for the two human-bred young ones.

In August 31, 1983, the two human-bred crested ibises were released. They flew about freely, and looked for food over the nearby paddy fields. In the evening they flew back to stay the night with their family in the nest. There appeared to be no differences between other crested ibises and the human-bred ones. The only dissimilarity was that when the breeder gave a signal to the flock of birds looking for food in the paddy fields, only the two human-bred ones elatedly flew over and wrested for the loaches in the pail held by the breeder. The others would stay gazing curiously from a distance.

Through the experiment with the two human-bred crested ibises in Yaojiagou, researchers have found that crested ibises are actually very gentle in nature and easily domesticated.

In a final 10-day period of March 1993, they put into practice the plan of "wild eggs, artificially hatched." They placed seven crested ibis eggs, taken from a nest in the wilds, into an incubator. Two of the eggs were hatched successfully in the same year. Since then, a plan for artificial incubation has developed very quickly. Professor Liu Yinzeng said: "Those concerned about the crested ibis might ask, would there be residual effects from inbreeding in the developed population generated by the seven crested ibises? I was also very worried about this myself, so I took great efforts to breed a few of the newly hatched birds separately in different places, to see the results after several generations. After the first crested ibis sent to the Beijing Zoo in 1981, we have started a new method for cage-bred populations. It is reassuring that up to now the problem of 'inbreeding' has not come up."

However, scientists have made certain advanced preparations. Japanese crested ibises originated in Yangxian, as do those in the Beijing Zoo. In March 2002, 60 crested ibises from Yangxian were transferred to Louguantai in Shaanxi's Zhouzhi County. Now the crested ibises in Louguantai have become the world's largest artificial population group. The numbers from breeding are geometrically increasing. In March 2007, with the growth of the artificial population, the Shaanxi Forestry Department for the first time carried out an experiment of releasing 10 pairs of human-bred crested ibises into the wilds. Scientists regard the experiment as having symbolic significance, pointing to a gradual shift for crested ibises from artificial breeding back to natural propagation.

"Nevertheless, in a sense, faith in the crested ibis not only lies in human attitudes but also in how the birds exert themselves evolutionarily." Guan Ke has his own opinion. He believes that, from a biological perspective, the crested ibis is an ancient species. It is an indisputable fact that its biological functions are regressive. This is also the reason why, under similar surroundings, little egrets, gray herons and other associated biological species have flourished in groups, while crested ibises vanished in great quantities. "Of course, when we observed and took photos of wild crested ibises in Yangxian, we also found some reassuring aspects. The viability of wild crested ibises is not so inferior to other birds. They are probably striving to adapt themselves to changes in the natural environment."

In original files from the Yangxian Crested Ibis Conservation Zone, are records of the arduous experiences of a crested ibis couple engaged in the process of natural propagation.

As a matter of fact, Yangxian's Jinjiahe can also be considered the place where the crested ibis was first rediscovered. In 1981, at Jinjiahe, a crested ibis nest was blown down by a gale and the eggs in it were broken, while at Yaojiagou people found two adult birds and three newly hatched ones. Hence the ring of honor fell on Yaojiagou as the first rediscovery site of crested ibises. However, the crested ibis couple in Jinjiahe has never given up its effort in propagation. In 1982, the same pair of crested ibises returned to build a nest again, and laid three eggs on a century-year-old Chinese scholar tree at Huanba, Jinjiahe. But local people cut down the tree, and once again the eggs were broken. The sorrowful pair flew to build a new nest at Nanchanggou nearby. Two eggs were laid, and then hatched in May. One of the young died of undernourishment. Two months later, the crested ibis pair left, discarding the nest, and the remaining young bird died during the departure. Then again they moved back to Jinjiahe and established a nest with four eggs in the spring of 1983. The records continue: "In the last 10-day period of April, at Silang Commune of Jinjiahe, the crested ibis laid four eggs but a crow smashed two of them. Later, to make up for the loss, two more eggs were laid. The breeding period was half a month later compared to that of the previous year. Propagation failed." After three failures in breeding their younger generation at Jinjiahe, the crested ibises left the village forever. They moved to Yaoping town's Sanchahe village and finally settled down there.

Sanchahe (Three-Fork River) village is situated at an altitude of 1,000 meters, with three streams originating in three barren gullies. The streams converge at the entrance of the village, hence its name. There are 36 households living by the streams in the village. They plant rice in summer in their three hectares of winter paddy fields. At the convergence of the three gullies grow 37 tall Qinggang trees, with five farmhouses nearby. In the surrounding area are emerald paddy fields. In April 1984, the crested ibises from Jinjiahe began to build a nest there. By the time they were discovered, they were already a family of five. The pair of birds, after enduring all sorts of hardships, had finally produced fruits of their love, but still misfortune followed them. In the middle of May one of the young birds fell down and died from starvation. So that year only two young ones survived.

Between 1984 and 1996, 10 of the younger generation of the crested ibis pair at Sanchahe lived on. Among them, five were rescued and bred in several households. Accompanied by ill fortune the crested ibis pair, sharing weal and woe, flew side by side for as many as 15 years or more. They demonstrated undauntable resolve in their struggle against nature. They were extraordinary compared with other natural living things. In 1998, the female bird died and their propagation stopped. The next year the lonely male acquired a new mate and continued procreation. However, most of the offspring ended up deformed or sickly. Yet, now the crested ibis population at Sanchahe is finally enjoying a time of fertility.

图书在版编目（CIP）数据

大熊猫与朱鹮的家园 / 崔黎丽编著；
邝文栋译. 一北京：外文出版社，2007
（国情故事丛书）
ISBN 978-7-119-05158-1

I.大... II.崔... III.①大熊猫 - 保护 - 概况 - 中国
②朱鹮 - 保护 - 概况 - 中国 IV. Q959.838 S863

中国版本图书馆 CIP 数据核字（2007）第 170965 号

策　　划	张锋锐 吴 涛
编　　著	崔黎丽
摄　　影	关 克 李 伟
责任编辑	余冰清 薛 芊
翻　　译	邝文栋
英文审定	May Yee 贺 军
封面及内文设计	天下智慧文化传播公司
制　　作	天下智慧文化传播公司
印刷监制	冯 浩

大熊猫与朱鹮的家园

*

© 外文出版社
外文出版社出版
（中国北京百万庄大街 24 号）
邮政编码 100037
北京外文印刷厂印刷
中国国际图书贸易总公司发行
（中国北京车公庄西路 35 号）
北京邮政信箱第 399 号 邮政编码 100044
2007 年(32 开)第 1 版
2007 年第 1 版 第 1 次印刷
（英）
ISBN 978-7-119-05158-1
10-E-3809P